POETRY, IN MOTION & STASIS

poems by

Carlo DiOrio

illustrations by

Joe Cairone

Finishing Line Press
Georgetown, Kentucky

POETRY, IN MOTION
& STASIS

ACKNOWLEDGMENTS

Kind of Blue and Lack-ees previously appeared in *CaKe, A Literary Journal.*
My Prayers and Grave Sight previously appeared in *California Quarterly.*
Ambition and Bed Time previously appeared in *The Artisan Magazine.*

Publisher: Leah Huete de Maines
Editor: Christen Kincaid
Cover Art and Design: Joe Cairone
Author Photo: Thomas Sayers Ellis

Order online: www.finishinglinepress.com
also available on amazon.com

Author inquiries and mail orders:
Finishing Line Press
PO Box 1626
Georgetown, Kentucky 40324
USA

Contents

Lighthouse 1

Ambition 3

Everything's Relative 5

Totem 7

My Prayers 9

Kind of Blue 11

Half Lives 13

Bed Time 15

Grave Sight 17

Carla and Pierre 19

Overtime 21

Cuddled 22

Remaindered 23

Skulking Coyotes 25

I Said 26

Lack-ees 27

Walking in El Lay 28

Hurricane Watch 29

Engulfed 31

LIGHTHOUSE

I carry my thoughts
like a pail of water.
Treading lightly,
and not, I follow a
seemingly endless
path, prodded by the
flickering beacon of

a far-off lighthouse.
My trek has coursed
through many years.
Though weary at times,
I am silently cheered
by the simple pleasure
of trudging the straight

and not-so-narrow
trail ahead. Often,
easily dozens of times,
I have ventured this
way and that to satisfy
devilish curiosity when
so inclined. Yet

purposeful stride by
purposeful stride,
largely without knowing,
I have lessened the
distance between me
and the lighthouse, not
to mention the vast,

sleeping ocean beyond.
I look forward to reaching
its once-remote shoreline,

where I casually will
empty the full contents
of my bucket into its
welcoming waters.

AMBITION

My ambition is to work
the words "Christ on a bike!"
into a poem. But no doubt I will
end up accomplishing nothing
much more than managing to eke

out a modicum of wonder as
I sit at sunset and spot just
the right amount of wantonly
accumulated cumulus to catch
a bit of orange
and pink
and gold.

EVERYTHING'S RELATIVE

Fighting it all the way, I finally submitted
near journey's end to a Hobson's choice that
led to my staying with Aunt Nettie & Uncle Al
instead of bedding down—during my parents'
weekend away—with Aunt Ronnie & Uncle
Nate. All packed up, my mother and father
left for Las Vegas right after dropping me at
the former's home rather than the latter's place
down the block. I'd totted up the pluses and
minuses of one domicile over the other, weighing
my decision for many miles but eventually
said just drop me at the first house we pass.

Many, many moons and more than a few
grown-up swoons later, I still have occasion
to think about family's multifaceted sameness:
the turkey dinner here, the baked ham
holiday there. But now, instead of relentless
tedium or stubborn torpor, this uniformly
predictable life strikes me more as luxurious
languor, as it follows so often the exhausting
chaos of worklife, of production quotas and
deadlines for "deliverables," of front-office
twits and back-office snits. Yes, today I find
that everything's relative, and fine.

TOTEM

The bird of paradise, the
White Bird of Paradise
is entirely green. But recently,
a long, tubular shoot has begun.
rising skyward (ceilingward).

Amid the huge flopping leaves
of this majestically stoic
Strelitzia nicolai appear the
silently boisterous beginnings
of a botanical birth—indoors,

by golly. True, this hearty gamer
will thrive indoors or out, makes
no matter in many climes. But
only the sodden soil of the great
outdoors is known to stimulate

any dependably predictable
production of its eponymous,
paradisiacal flowers. Certain
firm, often inscrutable, laws of
Nature, you see. Yet, obeying

nothing more than the nagging
of botanical rulebooks, climbs
a gem of a cocoon that would
seem to confirm its stubborn
insistence on rude health. So,

does this vigorous arising portend
only more green sheen, or might
we soon witness gentle genuflection
to the whimsy of flower power?
What we know for now: Game on!

MY PRAYERS

I think of my prayers
as colored balloons
let loose into open
skies above godknowswhat
floating aimlessly untethered
after nose punched blood
slapped forehead clutched
heart sigh sigh sigh joy
joy joy smiles and smiles
to go running this way and
that and devil-dogged days
of anything but a first
holy communion, or last,
filled not with hot air
but love.

KIND OF BLUE

Moods indigo or on the go, always
jukin' and jivin' to this polarity or that
depending on time, place, space, all that

jazz. And yet I'm soberly confident nothing
can send me too high or too low if I maintain
cruising altitude—closer to high than low? On

this day, landing gear locked, I softly touch down
(Hail Mary!) to change transport and float for many
miles until, Land ho! Unsinkable spirits spirit me away,

away from dark spirits of any sort. Now safely beached,
I notice a curious cormorant turn toward me quizzically, then
poke its beak briefly into the warm Gulf waters only then to take

sudden flight under azure open skies and soar off, off-camera. And
then and then and then, I beguine to sense a bit more contented,
more lasting sort of serenity, a kind of comfortable kind of blue.

HALF LIVES

Uncle Victor was a loveable guy,
if a bit "dim," as cruel contemporaries
might say. Always happy
to show a curious lad his proud
collection of 78-r.p.m. records
(Mario Lanza releases, mostly).
He'd be up for downing "a little something"
if offered a shot of festive spirits
yet never grew wobbly, simply sinking
a bit deeper into his front-porch easy chair.
But what to say of his younger years? Not sure
I ever bothered to inquire about my uncle's
schooling. Was he teased as a kid? Made
to work in the family tailor shops at an early age?
I'll never know and, truth be told, seldom wonder.
Still, I only knew one of my grandparents at all,
so the memory of my uncle's trove
of Italian vinyl is something, I suppose.

My grandkids' Grandad is someone they've known
without having to lavish special attention, no doubt
noticing his perfectly natural physical decline
and creeping mental lassitude. But of his
sturdy love of profession and "hardly working" past,
of any musical or literary tastes other than
the most obvious, of his tendency to talk to himself
at home since the passing of a longtime roommate

into cat heaven? *Nada* do they know, nor
care to imagine, I imagine. Still less do they know
of 8-year-old Susan Scanlon, who—on a dare,
no doubt—hopped out of her desk in Miss Mary's
third-grade classroom one resonantly sunny
afternoon to plant on my quickly blushing cheek
a peck of a kiss that grows ever-sweeter each time

recalled. Not that I have a clue regarding Susan's subsequent life, which I pray has been memorable.

BED TIME

Head hits pillow. Echoes
of song snippets lap the
subconscious. A distant
lover beckons once more,
weaving fragments of

past lives, of dreams,
of a dream. But an erudite
Aphrodite has no place
here. Only the slow, doltish
workings of a clock, speaking

now with the faucet: *Ticktick,
dripdrip, ticktick, dripdrip,
ticktick* ... up until the
dependably panicked alarm
clock shouts them down. But

what of the *silent* slumber-time
drama, those personal details
stowed godknowswhere until
another night, another dreamy
fragment to emerge, briefly.

GRAVE SIGHT

Standing before my
mother's yawning grave
I failed to hear the silent
fluttering of angels' wings.
Only the collective quiet
gave them away.

But I observed,
as if from another's eyes,
this: One brother flanked
by two, the eldest reaching out
with arms stretched wide to wrap
the shoulders of his younger,
quiescent siblings.

This gave rapid rise
to rampant storms of emotion,
none visible.

CARLA AND PIERRE

There's a photo of you and
a leashed Pierre, and it's
clear the moment is one of
unbridled joy for both of you.

It might have been your first
real chance to put your
shelter-rescue adoptee through
the paces at a local park

adorned with that scrawled,
"Clean Up After Your Dog"
sign. You with your happy
coat of many colors and him

displaying his signature
sheepdog shag, even though
Pierre was a poodle. As for
the guy behind the camera,

your erstwhile parent turned
weekend dad and weekday
dog-walker, it was also an
opportunity to dwell on nothing

but the best in our lives. The
self-censure would return soon
enough, but for these blessed hours
together—proud papa with

his dog-loving daughter and
a miniature poodle lapping up
outsized pampering—pure joy
shoved aside all opprobrium.

OVERTIME

Our elderly work on the existential
late shift, when worldly worries
abide, but a bit less openly.
The cumulative fatigue from their decades
of *sturm und drang* have diminished
their capacity to care extravagantly,
or at least about those concerns
of merely mortal import.

"She was ready to go …," we say
at wakes and memorials, speaking of
folks who live to a particularly ripe age.
One such nonagenarian—more simply
a nonna to several young adults at a
recent funeral—was remembered as
frequently muttering, "Why am I still here?"
Then she clocked out.

CUDDLE

I gather bracing books to
my breast and music to restore,
to bolster that often-flagging sense
that soon we will make it to shore.

Some friends, close family, even
casually welcomed guests who hold me
in momentary thrall, stir me to yearn for
all of this and more, just more. Simply more.

REMAINDERED

Flea-bitten, moth-eaten,
left for dead,
remains of the day
fill up my head.

At night comes sleep, though
short and fitful,
then morning's new start,
all clean and hopeful.

Best to let yesterday's
heartaches go for a song.

SKULKING COYOTES

Low to the ground, always. Their profile seems
to suggest a sense of intruding. Certainly,
that's how the residents of the mobile home park
view any coyote incursion. Yet it's tough to view

this hardy, hungry tribe as less native than
the aging pipefitters, housewives, retail clerks and
other members of the nation's retired diaspora who
have taken up residency hereabouts. The other

night I saw first one, then another and three and four
of the skulking critters scampering this way and that
through side lawns and sidewalks of the sleeping
neighborhood, making me sit upright and put my

long cigar down. Psst! You looking for your buddy?
He went that-a-way—no, no! The other yard, that's
where he cut through. Hmm, maybe he can still smell
his buddy; doesn't seem too concerned. Can't be that

the four of them have traveled together only to lose
one another right in front of my place. Friends, yes,
that's what I need, a pack of friends with whom
I can run wild, or at least smoke a cigar, jauntily.

I SAID

I said I was angry
and grew smaller.

I moaned I was bored
and grew calloused.

I gave voice to hate
and grew cankers.

I said I loved
and grew.

LACK-EES

We stuff our self with work
and then explode into fragments of
fun-seeking weekend "activities." Why? To
keep our minds, our mind, away from the hollow
core that plunges ever so downward. Downy thoughts
may comfort us when darkness creeps, but for how long?
How high the walls of our fort of insecurity, easily scalable
by almost any sort of foe we know, or don't. It seems the only
recourse left may be to find the means of finding—what, exactly?
Joy ...

WALKING IN EL LAY

Oh, to walk lightly through
each day, I say, then recall
when youth prescribed the
rush of running recklessly
through the drizzle of daily
indignities, giddily defying
the gravity of consequence.
Life caught between a hard
rock place in time and cool
jazz go lightly fadeouts. And
I espy with my brittle sighs a
reticence to rummage through
dusty lore, now shotgun-wedded
to a measured pace with days
drawn slow by nothing so much
as a pregnant sense of essence.

HURRICANE WATCH

The first gust blows through the
Florida room so unexpectedly, a
brazen home invasion one full day
ahead of the much-anticipated storm
strike. And then things go quiet again,
the hurricane's sweep still nowhere near

as yet, let alone the plodding beast's eye.
But the bold blast out of nowhere demands
attention, sets nerves on edge, announces
that watchful measures must be maintained,
for much more wind and rain and general
mayhem are certain to come soon enough,

and one doesn't know when or how that
next incursion will arrive. So, jitters,
yes, so very common. But one mustn't
get twisted in knots for nothing. So,
sufficient caffeine to stay alert but not to
fuel the latent anxiety further. Quite soon,

perhaps, there will be plenty of something,
marking the storm's arrival and brusque,
indeterminate residency. And then there will be
more plenty of something. And then in fits
and starts, or with startling suddenness,
this, too, will pass. Eventfully, eventually.

ENGULFED

Sleeping, I float through a
bobbing slurry of decayed
SIM cards, frayed USB cords,
knotted coaxial cable. Waking,
I am anything but awake,
more or less sleepwalking
amid faint echoes of my
techno-phobic nocturnal
travels. Happily, I am
pulled in the direction of
morning birdsong, plodding
a path that opens eventually
into an expanse of verdant
wonder: a park populated
by no one other than some
seabirds flown in to peck away
at the sun-specked grass.
Trudging happily just a bit
further, I watch as the sky
opens around me, then wraps
my every sense in its azure
wonderment. And finally,
miles and smiles away from
thoughts of info-puking screens,
from devilish "devices," from the
quenchless thirst of battery-chargers,
I find the Gulf of Mexico.
And many, many more seabirds.
A passing dolphin applauds
my providential escape.

Carlo DiOrio is a career journalist whose poems have appeared in publications including *California Quarterly, The Artisan Magazine* and *CaKe, A Literary Journal.* A Philadelphia native, he lived for many years in Los Angeles and now resides in Largo, Florida. DiOrio's poetry draws on themes such as nature, music, aging and other life passages. He occasionally hangs such themes on geographical hooks and often employs wordplay, though at other times the simplicity of his poems show a dotted-line connection to his long career in journalism.

Joe Cairone is a former landscape architect and a Pennsylvania-based artist who works in watercolor, oils, pen & ink and other mediums. His mentors have included Karl J. Kuerner of the Brandywine Conservancy in Chadds Ford, Pa.